Workbook

For

Brianna Wiest's

The Mountain Is You

Smart Reads

Note to readers:
This is an unofficial workbook for Brianna
Wiest's "The Mountain Is You" designed to
enrich your reading experience. The original
book can be purchased on Amazon.

The information contained in this book has been compiled
from sources deemed reliable and it is accurate to the best

Download Your Free Gift

As a way to say "Thank You" for being a fan of our series, I've included a free gift for you:

Brain Health: How to Nurture and Nourish Your Brain For Top Performance

Go to www.smart-reads.com to get your FREE book.

The Smart Reads Team

Table of Contents

Overview of *The Mountain Is You*

The Mountain is You: Transforming Self-Sabotage Into Self-Mastery written by Brianna Wiest is about how we play a role in the outcomes of our lives. It goes into depth about how we must develop a deep understanding of ourselves in order to overcome the challenges we face in life and eventually master ourselves. Most of us need to reach rock bottom before we can truly recognize that we must master and understand ourselves.

One of the mountains we must overcome is self-sabotage. Self-sabotage can be an act of self-preservation and self-protection. If we are unaware of why we self-sabotage and the ways we self-sabotage, we will never be able to move past our self-sabotaging behaviors.

Self-mastery eventually comes when we reflect deeply on ourselves, and we use the insights we've learned to better ourselves and our outcomes.

Chapter 1: The Mountain Is You

Chapter 1 talks about how we play a part in holding ourselves back through self-sabotage.

Self-sabotage can be a way of protecting ourselves from the unknown, even if the outcome might be a good or desired one.

Despite what most might think, self-sabotage can be a way for us to cope and protect ourselves from difficult or overwhelming outcomes. Self-sabotage can be hard to spot at times, especially when we are self-sabotaging to stay safe or comfortable.

Self-sabotage can be formed from attachments, illogical fears, negative associations, and outdated, unexamined belief systems. Our beliefs (whether real or not) eventually form attachments that we view the world through. For example, if you believe that in order to do well at your job you have to be extremely nice to everyone, you will become attached to that belief. That attachment might then cause you to become irrationally fearful of saying no or creating boundaries in your workplace.

Self-sabotage can also be formed from the unfamiliar and unknown. For example, if you're accustomed to terrible partners in relationships, you might be uncomfortable being in a healthy, positive relationship. This chapter introduces Gay Hendricks' idea called the "upper limit." It is the idea that we each have our own tolerance for how much happiness we can handle. When we reach our upper limit, we most likely will find ourselves engaging in self-sabotage behaviors.

To overcome and challenge our self-sabotaging ways, we need to accept our role and take accountability for our actions.

We can no longer deny our part, and we must accept that life is what we make it. We have to find the determination to want better for ourselves and to know that we can change if we choose to.

Chapter Summary

Key Points:

- We hold ourselves back through self-sabotage.

- Self-sabotage is a way to protect ourselves from the unknown and unfamiliar, even if the unfamiliar is something that we desire or something that will make us happy. Self-sabotage can be triggered when we reach our upper limit.

- We are responsible for learning about ourselves and the ways we self-sabotage. We are accountable for our own lives and actions. We must do the work in order to face ourselves and change for the better.

Questions:

- What are ways in which you've self-sabotaged in the past?

_____
_____
_____

- What are some of your upper limits?

_____
_____
_____

- What are difficult truths for you to accept about yourself and your life?

_____
_____
_____

Action Plan:

1. Reflect on your self-limiting beliefs and fears.

2. Journal about the questions above.

3. List your top 5 goals for the next year. After listing your goals, create a plan for each goal.

4. Journal and envision what your life will look like when you achieve the 5 goals. Reflect and describe in detail how you will feel. Think about who will be in your life, and what other goals you might accomplish because of your 5 goals.

Chapter 2: There's No Such Thing as Self-Sabotage

Chapter 2: There's No Such Thing as Self-Sabotage goes deeper into explaining self-sabotage.

Self-sabotage can happen when our subconscious and conscious are at odds.

You might have a lot of dreams and aspirations, but you haven't taken action on any of your dreams or aspirations. Chapter 2 pushes us to ask why. The truth might be that we are comfortable and feel safe having issues or problems in our lives. We are attached to the current state of our life, and to ask ourselves why would mean we would have to take accountability for what it currently is.

What does self-sabotage look like? How can we resolve it?

Resistance

We usually find ourselves resisting positive change in our lives. We hold back from things that could make us happy, successful, etc. We fear disappointment so much that we are willing to resist the "right" things in our lives in order to avoid possible failure.

How can we resolve it?

We can resolve resistance by reflecting on what it is we want and why we want it. We also have to examine and confront any beliefs that are holding us back from what we want.

Hitting your upper limit

Your upper limit is basically your tolerance for the good and happiness in your life. When we've reached and gone beyond our upper limit, we start to self-sabotage because of how unfamiliar and uncomfortable it feels.

How can we resolve it?

We resolve this by having patience with ourselves and learning to adjust to our new normal. We can also resolve this by reflecting on why reaching our upper limit makes us feel uncomfortable and what ways we can work through the feelings.

Uprooting

Constantly quitting jobs, ending relationships, moving from place to place, etc. is uprooting. If you find yourself starting fresh all the time instead of resolving the problem or facing the consequences for your actions, then you are engaging in uprooting. It can be a way to distract ourselves from the real issues in our lives. When we are busy starting new things all the time, we will not have energy or time to face the real problems or issues in our life.

How can we resolve it?

We resolve this by examining our behaviors in the past and figuring out the pattern for it. We have to hold ourselves accountable for the uprooting pattern and dig deep to figure out what it is we are searching for and/or avoiding.

Perfectionism

Perfectionism is our deep desire for everything to be perfect and exactly the way we want it to be. Perfectionism can end up holding us back from moving forward and taking action. With perfectionism, we get caught up in other people's perceptions of our actions instead of how we can take action.

How can we resolve it?

We can resolve this by simply doing. The more we take action and do, the more progress we make. Taking action quiets down the need to be perfect.

Limited Emotional Processing Skills

We hold ourselves back from not fully processing and expressing our emotions. Our emotions will stay bottled up if we do not process them. Even though they are bottled up, that does not mean that they have disappeared. Our feelings are simply waiting to reveal themselves.

How can we resolve it?

We can resolve limited emotional processing by clarifying what happened; validating our feelings, and deciding how we want to move forward.

Justification

We can't justify our lack of action through our intention. We can have intentions to create a wonderful business, but without action, our intention remains a thought. We self-sabotage when we measure our success through intentions and not only outcomes. We make ourselves feel better through excuses.

How can we resolve it?

We can resolve this by actually measuring outcomes (not intentions). We can also resolve this through discipline and holding ourselves accountable to follow through on our plans.

Disorganization

We self-sabotage by not keeping a clean and organized environment. A disorganized environment is distracting, and it can be difficult to feel creative and focused. When our space is organized, our minds will also feel organized and calm. When our minds feel good, we are able to do good work.

How can we resolve it?

We can resolve this by taking time to clean up and declutter our environment. We can also resolve this by creating systems that will help us keep organized, as well. For example, we could invest in a storage system.

Attachment to What You Really Don't Want

Our lack of motivation and commitment does not always stem from fears. It can be because we simply don't want to do something. Some of our attachments come from past beliefs or other people's opinions. These attachments do not serve us, but we hold on to them.

How can we resolve it?

We can resolve this by questioning our reasonings and motivations, especially when we are finding it difficult to stay committed and motivated. Also, we can resolve this by accepting ourselves for who we are in the current moment, and letting go of who we are not anymore.

Judging Others

When we judge others, we are ultimately judging ourselves. When you pass judgment on others, you are also creating a standard for yourself to live up to. Judging others also uses up our time and energy in a wasteful way.

How can we resolve it?

We can resolve this by having more grace for others, and accepting others for who they are. We can also choose to not pass judgment on others.

Pride

Our pride can hold us back from living the life we truly want. Our pride can get in the way of fully accepting ourselves and our desires.

How can we resolve it?

We can resolve this by letting go of how we think we should be and act, and accepting ourselves for who we truly are.

Guilt of Succeeding

Some people feel guilty because of how much money they have or how many great things they have accomplished. Guilt can lead to self-sabotaging of our success and opportunities. It can lead us to playing small and not going after what we truly want.

How can we resolve it?

We can resolve this by recognizing the guilt we have, and by further examining how we can use the wealth we have to help others.

Fear of Failing

The fear of failure can cause us to not go after our goals. It can make us feel stuck in a situation.

How can we resolve it?

We can resolve this by examining our fear and understanding that failure can happen, especially when we try something new. We can also remind ourselves that not trying leads to 100% failure.

Downplaying

We downplay our success and achievement for a variety of reasons. Downplaying can cause us to not feel as impressed or happy about our achievements. We do a disservice to ourselves when we play small.

How can we resolve it?

We can resolve this by celebrating our achievements and other people's achievements. We can also resolve this by accepting when someone congratulates or compliments us.

Unhealthy Habits

We self-sabotage when our goals and habits do not align. You can't achieve a healthy sleep schedule by choosing to stay up late every night. Similarly, you'll have a more difficult time exercising if you smoke cigarettes often. Our habits help shape the quality of our lives.

How can we resolve it?

We can resolve this by exploring and figuring out what being healthy means to you and setting health goals.

Being "Busy"

We can self-sabotage by having a busy schedule. Sometimes we over-complicate our schedule because it makes us feel more accomplished or important. We also over-complicate our schedule in order to avoid more pressing issues.

How can we resolve it?

We can resolve this by reviewing our current schedule and examining our productivity and ways to speed up processes & tasks. Also, creating free time in our schedule can help.

Spending Time With the Wrong People

Who we hang out with can affect our lifestyles. The people we surround ourselves with can help build us up or break us down.

How can we resolve it?

We can resolve this by connecting with people that inspire us and make us feel good. We can choose to invest in the relationships that bring positive energy into our lives.

Worrying About Irrational Fears and Least Likely Circumstances

We can self-sabotage by using our time and energy to worry and overthink about unlikely scenarios.

How can we resolve it?

We can resolve this by reflecting on the reasons behind our worries and fears. We can take it deeper by feeling the feelings that come up.

Understanding self-sabotaging behaviors can help us know when you're in a cycle of self-sabotage. If you find yourself worrying about outcomes you do not want or avoiding what is going on in your life, then you are most likely in a cycle of self-sabotage. If you find yourself trying to impress people whose opinions don't matter to you or you are trying to assure people that you're okay when you're not, you're most likely self-sabotaging. Being able to identify these signs will help get you out of the cycle.

We should also spend time identifying our subconscious commitments. Wiest describes our core commitment is our primary intention for our life. We need to develop an understanding of our subconscious commitments so that we can understand our behaviors and actions. We can also figure out what it is we truly want.

Confronting our self-sabotaging behaviors and being honest with ourselves is not easy. Breaking through self-sabotage and changing will feel uncomfortable and overwhelming. We naturally want to seek out comfort and safety. Change is uncomfortable, and the unknown can make us feel unsafe.

We can overcome self-sabotage by taking action and continuing forward despite how uncomfortable, overwhelmed, and scared we feel.

Chapter Summary

Key Points:

- Self-sabotage can manifest in a variety of ways, such as resistance, downplaying, pride, etc. If we recognize these self-sabotaging behaviors, we can resolve them.

- Confronting and overcoming self-sabotage is difficult and can make us feel like we are at odds with ourselves. Instead of getting over these feelings, we need to question and reflect on them.

- One of the biggest lessons in overcoming self-sabotage is disconnecting our actions and feelings. Our feelings do not always reflect what is going on in reality. We might feel extremely overwhelmed, anxious, and uncomfortable when challenging our self-sabotaging behaviors, but that is not an indicator that we are doing the wrong thing.

Questions:

- What self-sabotaging behaviors are more prominent in your life?

_____
_____
_____

- How can you overcome your self-sabotaging behaviors?

_____
_____
_____

- How do you normally handle change?

_____
_____
_____

Action Plan:

1. Reflect on the self-sabotage list.

2. Create a list of tools and ways you can use to help overcome the behaviors.

3. Journal and reflect on how your feelings have affected your actions in the past.

4. Create a plan for one goal you want to accomplish by the end of the year.

Chapter 3: Your Triggers Are the Guides to Your

Chapter 3 talks about how our triggers can help us develop a deeper understanding of ourselves. The chapter goes over how we can interpret and figure out what our negative emotions are trying to teach us.

How to Interpret Negative Emotions:

- **Anger** can transform our lives and cause us to take action. Instead of getting aggressive when we feel angry, we should use our anger to motivate change.

- **Sadness** must be felt and processed. Otherwise, it builds up and can become a problem. Sadness is completely okay to feel, and it usually happens when we lose someone or something or when we encounter disappointment.

- **Guilt** requires reflection and accountability. Sometimes guilt is not related to what we are currently experiencing. Guilt can come from your past, especially surrounding your childhood.

- **Embarrassment** is usually from when we act in a way that we are not pleased with. When embarrassment isn't processed or simply felt, it can lead to feelings of shame.

- **Jealousy** usually presents itself as anger or passing judgment, but if you take a closer look, you'll find that it is most likely hiding feelings of sadness or discontent. We are usually jealous of others that have something or have accomplished something that we want.

- **Resentment** can arise when we are disappointed in someone not meeting our expectations. We can release resentment by accepting people for who they are.

- **Regret** manifests when we are unhappy about an action we took or about not taking action. Wiest mentions that we usually tend to regret the action we did not take. Regret can be used as motivation to change and to work on our goals.

- **Chronic fear** mainly manifests from thoughts in our head and past trauma. If we do not let go of our fears, it can destroy our lives. We must accept fear to overcome it. If we fight it or try to control it, we will continue the cycle of fear.

We need to validate our needs to move away from our patterns of self-sabotage. The more we feel our feelings and validate them, the better we will be at letting them go. Our feelings and our mind are trying to communicate with us. If we can recognize how we are self-sabotaging, we can dig deeper into what our subconscious mind is trying to tell us.

For example, if you are self-sabotaging with unhealthy eating habits, your subconscious mind might be trying to tell you that you need balance in your life. You need to eat healthily but allow for some treats here and there. Or your subconscious mind could be telling you that you are unhappy about something in your life, and you're using food as a way to satiate that feeling.

Another example of self-sabotaging is spending too much time on social media. Your subconscious mind could be telling you that you need to face what's happening in your life and not run away or numb yourself to it.

By understanding ourselves, we can follow our instincts. We all have a gut instinct. We should not confuse this instinct with being able to tell the future.

An instinct is what takes place in the present moment.

If you find yourself responding to something that is not happening right now, then that most likely *is not* your gut instinct. If you find yourself responding to what's happening in the present moment, then that most likely *is* your gut instinct.

Your gut instinct is responding to what is going on right here and now. For example, if you're crossing the street and a car starts to speed up, your instinct will most likely alert you to get out of harm's way. Your instinct is knowing what to do in the present moment. Your instinct is different from fear because it is not alarming or loud. Your instinct is quiet and calm.

Your instinct goes hand-in-hand with your intuition. The more in-tune we are with ourselves, the better we can listen to our intuition. Intuitive thoughts are not intrusive thoughts.

Intuitive thoughts motivate you to keep pushing forward; offer you a rational perspective, and open you up to a wide range of ideas and possibilities. Intrusive thoughts cause fear; are overwhelming, and make assumptions.

We can learn how to take care of ourselves beyond our basic needs when we develop our self-awareness and learn to trust our instinct and intuition.

Chapter Summary

Key Points:

- Negative feelings can trigger us to change and grow. We can build self-awareness and self-mastery when we understand our emotions and feel them.

- We need to validate ourselves, our needs, and our feelings to get past self-sabotaging behaviors.

- Our instinct and intuition get better the more we listen and act on them.

Questions:

- Choose a feeling from the negative emotions list above. Think about a time that you have felt that emotion. What is that feeling trying to communicate with you? How can you use it to overcome self-sabotage?

_____

_____

_____

- When have you listened to your intuition? What ended up happening?

_____

_____

_____

- When have you gone against your gut instinct? What ended up happening?

_____

_____

_____

Action Plan:

1. Reflect on the negative emotions list above. Think about some of your experiences with the feelings listed.

2. Think about moments when you might have invalidated your feelings.

3. Choose one moment to go back to and to meditate on it.

4. In your meditation, communicate with your past self and validate yourself and your feelings.

Chapter 4: Building Emotional Intelligence

Chapter 4 explains emotional intelligence and our brains in depth.

Emotional intelligence is the ability to recognize, assess, use and control our emotions.

Understanding our emotions is a key part of understanding ourselves. When we understand our feelings, we can gain an understanding of how they affect our minds and bodies and vice versa. Our mind, body, and spirit are all connected. They all affect each other in one way or another.

Our brains have the ability to sabotage achieving our goals or getting what we want. The dopamine wears off when we get what we want leading us to want more. This can lead us to self-sabotage when we are close to getting what we want.

Being in the state of wanting is easier than being in the state of having.

The state of having can lead to the state of losing. Therefore, because having might lead to losing, we feel more comfortable remaining in the state of wanting. Actually having something brings up fears of what could possibly happen if we lose it.

The fear of losing what we have is scary enough to derail our progress and to cause us not to want something.

Our brains are in charge of what we pay attention to and what we ignore. They are constantly scanning for what is familiar and bringing that information to the forefront. The thoughts that we currently think do not have to be the thoughts that we always think. We can change our thoughts and mindset. We must learn about our brains and the ways we think in order to master our thoughts, actions, and feelings. What we give our attention to and commit our time to will ultimately affect our life.

Change happens in microshifts. Microshifts are small actions that we take. Long-lasting change is not caused by one big action, but many small actions. We do not come to realizations based on one thought but on many thoughts and perspective shifts.

Change is sustainable when it comes in small doses.

Otherwise, our brains can discern a big change as threatening, causing us to revert to our old ways. We have to give our brains time to catch up and accept our changes by changing gradually and with small actions. Daily habits compound and become big life changes.

This chapter also highlights how complex the human mind is and how it is antifragile. Antifragile means that the human mind is prone to rise to the challenge when it is faced with adversity.

The mind subconsciously seeks out challenges, especially when we try to avoid them.

Your mind might also create problems in your life in order to face a challenge. Instead of shielding ourselves and our minds from difficulties and challenges, we should push ourselves outside of our comfort zone in positive and helpful ways. Uncomfortability does not mean that something isn't right for us or that we made the wrong decision. We must let go of that notion.

We must also accept that with new experiences (good or bad) comes a lot of emotions, especially stress. Change is stressful for everyone, and we must learn how to handle the stress that comes with it. In order to grow, we must get comfortable with the uncomfortable.

When making changes, most of us go through adjustment shock which can show up as feeling irritable, anxious, upset, etc. If we do not have self-awareness about why we feel this way when it comes to stress, our minds will become afraid when it comes to us succeeding or reaching our goals. This fear might then cause our mind to go back to our old ways before the stress.

What is psychic thinking?

Psychic thinking can be defined as a cognitive bias that is usually showcased in the following ways:

- **Confirmation**: Our brains are wired to filter through the information according to our experiences, thoughts, and beliefs. Our brains will actively seek out information that supports our beliefs and previous experiences. For example, if you think a friend is never prompt, you might miss and not remember the times that they were on time.

- **Extrapolation**: Our minds can convince us that how things are now is how they will always be. Extrapolation is when we believe that our past and current feelings can predict how we will feel in the future.

- **Spotlighting**: It is the idea that we are being watched and judged constantly. Spotlighting is when we think that everyone's thoughts and actions revolve around us. It is when we think that people can recall specific situations or mistakes we've made.

Not only do we need to be aware of our biases, we also need to be aware of logical lapses. A logical lapse is getting caught up in one part of your thoughts that you end up stuck in a loop. Logical lapses usually come with anxiety and feelings of worry.

When we feel anxious about an outcome, we tend to worry about it. When we worry, we short circuit our brains from fully processing the situation and coming up with a different outcome.

To combat logical lapses, we have to face the worry or fear that we have. For example, if you're fearful of public speaking, you can sign up to read to kindergarteners to help expose yourself to that fear. The more you face your fear, the easier it is to overcome it. Mental fortitude is when you believe you can handle whatever comes your way.

Faulty inferences are also holding you back from confronting your fears and achieving your goals. A faulty inference is when you come to a false conclusion based on real evidence. For example, generalizing or stereotyping a group of people because of the few encounters you've had with them. You can resolve faulty inference by taking notice of when it happens and working to correct it.

Our minds try to predict the future in order to keep us safe. One way we do that is through worrying. Worrying is a way to give us the illusion of control. We cannot predict the future, but if we think and worry about the worst possible outcome, it somehow feels helpful. Worrying does not help; it hurts. We need to recognize when we are worrying and learn to cope.

Chapter Summary

Key Points:

- Our brains are wired to protect us, but there are times when its protection is not conducive to our growth and success. Our brains can perceive new experiences as scary which can cause us not to move forward with making changes.

- Change is stressful. Changing in microshifts can help with the longevity and success of our changes.

- Psychic thinking, logical lapses, faulty inferences, and worrying are all ways our brain uses to predict the future and keep us safe. We need to be aware of these ways of thinking to recognize when we are implementing them.

Questions:

- What changes in your life have been stressful? How did the stress manifest?

_____
_____
_____

- What are healthy ways that you cope with stress?

_____
_____
_____

- What types of thinking (psychic thinking, logical lapses, etc) have you experienced in the past? Were you able to recognize what was happening?

_____
_____
_____

- What are the worries that you can let go of today?

_____
_____
_____

Action Plan:

1. Think about a fear or worry that you have been experiencing right now. Reflect on where that fear comes from.

2. Create a step-by-step plan to overcome that fear or worry.

3. Start on the first step from the plan you created.

Chapter 5: Release the Past

Chapter 5 is about processing and letting go of the past. Letting go happens differently for everyone. It is a process that we have to be willing to start for it to be successful. We cannot force ourselves to let go of past experiences, feelings, regrets, etc. if we are not ready to do so. Letting go takes time. Letting go is necessary to let go to overcome self-sabotage.

The Psychological Trick to Release Old Experiences

We can use the psychological trick of meeting with our younger selves to let go of the past. To do this, you can imagine being with your younger self during a rough time in your past. While you are together, imagine imparting wisdom to your younger self.

Imagine yourself giving them advice and creating a plan together. Imagine yourself letting them know it will all be okay. By meeting with your younger self, you can release old attachments, and also gain our power back.

Letting go of the past also requires accepting and validating how it affected you. It is fully experiencing the feelings and emotions that you might have held yourself back from experiencing previously.

Like the past, we must also let go of unrealistic ideals and expectations. We might end up finding that a lot of our ideals and expectations for ourselves no longer align with our present selves. We must be content here and now.

We must let go of what we think life should be and accept ourselves and our life for what it truly is.

We must get comfortable with the uncomfortable parts of ourselves and our lives. When we start to be our true selves at this moment, our lives will change.

We must also accept that what is meant for us will always be for us. If something is not right for us, it will not be in our life. It might come into our lives, but it will never stay. It will eventually find its way out of our life. What is not right for us will never feel good.

We all have an inner knowing when something is not right for us. Sometimes we choose to ignore that feeling, but it eventually surfaces, and it can be difficult to ignore. We must accept when something is not right for us, and let it go.

We must also reflect on our trauma to recover from it. Trauma can be described as an experience that has made you feel distressed and/or fearful, and from which you have not recovered.

Trauma removes your connection to the feeling of safety.

After we've experienced trauma, our brains will most likely perceive everything as a threat. This might happen for a short time, but the aftereffects can be long-lasting.

Trauma can affect our brains and the development of our brains, especially in the parts where we process stress. The amygdala, hippocampus, and prefrontal cortex are where we process stress in the brain. Trauma can stop our brains from fully processing memories which can lead us to not fully remembering an experience or only remembering the parts that add to our cognitive bias. It can also make it difficult for us to handle and feel a wide variety of emotions. Making it so that we only feel certain emotions, specifically "negative" emotions. Trauma can affect our ability to plan and set goals for the future.

Trauma can leave our body in a fight-or-flight state causing us to be hypervigilant and sensitive to stimuli. Our body stops developing in the fight-or-flight state which can cause us to be stagnant. In order to release our trauma, we need to accept our trauma, and we need to come up with a plan for when we are faced with the same situation. Not only is trauma held in our bodies, but we also can hold emotions in our bodies.

An emotional backlog happens when we do not accept and feel our feelings. We need to physically feel our feelings to let go of them. Otherwise, they remain in our bodies – building up until we cannot ignore them. An emotional backlog can manifest physically as a stomachache, headache, heartache, etc. Eventually, the backlog starts to build up and force its way out.

How to get rid of an emotional backlog:

- **Start meditating to feel.** Use meditation to sit with and feel your emotions. Meditation is not always calm or quiet. It can be uncomfortable and chaotic. It can be a way for us to get comfortable with the uncomfortable. Meditation can help us start feeling and stop repressing.

- **Use breath scans to find residual tension in the body.** Breathe in and out slowly while scanning your body for any aches and pains or feelings of tension. Take note of the parts of your body that you notice feelings of tension or pain. Reflect later on what could be the cause of the pain.

- **Sweat, move, cry.** Release your emotions through actions. Your emotions must be released in one way or the other. Spend time releasing your emotions in ways that are healthy and productive for you.

Healing our minds allows us to tap into our true selves. When we heal our minds, we return to our natural, free state. Healing requires you to feel all of your emotions and accept them for what they are. Healing requires you to take an in-depth look at your life and to be honest about what you need to change without passing judgment. Healing requires trust, transparency, and non-judgment. Healing requires that we face the dark, shadow parts of ourselves, and make peace with those parts.

Healing is not easy. Healing is difficult and requires a commitment to doing the work. It requires discipline and time. Healing can be extremely rewarding, and it can lead us to become the best and most authentic version of ourselves. Healing means that we accept our past experiences for what they are, and that we accept the person we are today. Healing means that we can look to the future with optimism and not fear or worry. It means that you can accept and be comfortable with yourself here and now.

When we heal, we move forward. We allow ourselves to simply be.

Our healing and commitment to moving forward needs to be based on our desires, and not on getting revenge.

We will not find success when we base our healing on revenge. If our desire is to gain recognition in order to make someone regret how they treated us, then our healing is based on revenge. We have to let go of the need for revenge in order to fully heal.

Moving forward means shedding the old to make space for the current (the new). It is finding closure in your past, and to let go of needing other people's approval. Moving forward is finding approval within ourselves, and loving our lives for what they truly are and how they feel.

Chapter Summary

Key Points:

- We must face and accept our trauma in order to overcome it. Oftentimes, we are unable to accept how much an experience has affected us which prolongs the healing process. When we are able to accept our trauma, we can let go of it.

- Trauma and an emotional backlog can affect our minds and bodies. It can cause us to not fully feel our emotions; to be fearful of the future, and to feel aches and pains in our bodies.

- We need to release our emotions in physical ways in order to alleviate the emotional backlog.

- Healing is freeing. Although healing is not easy, it is rewarding.

Questions:

- What traumas are you still holding on to?

_____
_____
_____

- What can you do to face and let go of your traumas?

_____
_____
_____

- What actions can you take this month to get rid of your emotional backlog?

_____
_____
_____

- What parts of you are still unhealed?

_____
_____
_____

Action Plan:

1. Reflect and journal on a trauma that you have not confronted yet.

2. List ways to face and accept the trauma (e.g. writing a letter to your past self, writing a letter to the person that hurt you, etc.).

3. Meditate on your feelings surrounding the trauma and let go of it.

4. Reflect and journal about your meditation.

Chapter 6: Building a New Future

Chapter 6: Building a New Future covers what happens after you confront, accept, release, and heal.

We must fully move on from the past to build a new future. Once we overcome the work of healing from the past, learning from our trauma, and developing a deep self-awareness, we can move on to creating our future and planning for our future outcomes. This chapter covers how we can create and connect with our best potential future selves.

How to connect with your highest potential self:

- **Face the fear first.** Start a meditation practice, and imagine yourself sitting in a room that is comfortable. Imagine you feel calm and content. Then invite a future version of yourself to talk with you, specifically the highest version of yourself. During this conversation, take note of the details. Be open to receiving advice from yourself.

- **Notice how your future self looks.** Pay attention to everything going on during your conversation, such as: how your future self looks, how they act, how they speak, etc. This can help you create a blueprint for the actions you should take.

- **Ask for guidance.** Don't get caught up in specifics or asking daunting questions. Instead, remain open when asking yourself for guidance. Be open to what they have to share with you.

- **Imagine them handing you the "keys" to your new life.** Imagine them handing you things that are associated with your future life, such as your future career goals, your bank account information, your relationships, etc.

Another way to start building a new future is to let go of the past. Trauma manifests and is stored in our bodies. If trauma is not dealt with, it can start to show up in our daily lives. To help from trauma, we must reflect on what caused the trauma. Then we need to restore a sense of safety in our lives.

We can do this by exposing ourselves to healthy experiences. If we were traumatized by an unhealthy friendship, we can restore our sense of safety by creating healthy friendships. If we were traumatized by poor parenting, we have to learn how to reparent ourselves and reinvent our past experiences. Lastly, we need to accept that we can't predict the future. We have to stop relying on our thoughts and feelings to predict or control our actions.

To become the most powerful version of ourselves, we have to learn who that person is. We can start by visualizing our most powerful selves to get a sense of who they are, what their habits are, and how they behave. We need to reflect on how we will feel as our most powerful selves. Then we must learn and become aware of what our weaknesses and shortcomings are. By being aware of these things, we can seek out support or find ways to improve.

We must be okay with not being liked. We will be judged and at times, we will be disliked. We must get comfortable with the idea that not everyone is going to like or accept us. We also must accept that it is okay for people to dislike us. It is not our responsibility to convince others to like us, especially when we do not act in a way that is malicious or condescending.

We must be confident to act with a purpose. Our purpose is ever changing. If our dreams do not align with our purpose, we will not feel motivated to pursue or commit to them. Being clear on what we want and what it will take to be our most powerful selves will help us find our inner power. Finding our inner power will help us accomplish great things.

Lastly, we must also do the inner work. We must reflect on our life lessons and how we can be and do better. We must reflect on our triggers and what they are trying to teach us. We must reflect on our traumas and feel what we had previously suppressed. Doing the inner work means becoming comfortable with who we are and becoming confident in how we move about the world.

Emotional validation for ourselves and others can be an incredibly powerful tool. Validating someone's feelings means that you are saying it is okay for them to feel that way. It doesn't mean you necessarily agree with it or that it is the correct way to feel. It simply means that, as humans, it is okay to feel however we feel. It is okay to express emotions. We don't always have to understand why we feel a certain way in order to validate our feelings. We just have to let ourselves feel it.

Invalidating our feelings could cause us to seek validation from others instead.

It can cause us to not feel safe or comfortable expressing our feelings even to ourselves. The reality is we need to validate our feelings in order to feel and move past them. Otherwise, invalidating our feelings could end up leading to self-sabotaging behaviors.

When we process and validate our feelings, we allow them to flow out of us and to be released. If we do not validate our feelings, it can cause them to build up making them more difficult to eventually accept and release. Not only are we going to have to deal with the feeling, but we will then have to deal with the invalidation of that feeling.

Validating our feelings is ultimately a lot easier than suppressing or making it so that we do not feel that way. When we invalidate our feelings, we might find ourselves crying out for help in other ways. We might find ourselves acting out in order to receive validation. Not validating our feelings can ultimately lead to self-sabotaging behaviors.

We can validate our feelings through journaling or meditating. Journaling and meditation can help us hold space for ourselves and our feelings. It can assist us in processing our feelings and responding to them. We can also learn how to validate our feelings through validating other people's feelings. When we feel for others, we create the capacity to feel for ourselves.

Another way to support and build ourselves up is clarifying our principles. We need to get clear on our principles. Otherwise, we end up living by other people's principles or old principles that we once held.

A principle is a truth that we hold that is foundational to parts of our lives. Principles can be seen as personal instructions and directions on how you want to lead your life. We need principles for the different aspects of our lives, such as money, relationships, self-care, career, etc.

An example of a money principle could be to save 5% of your income every month. Or a relationship principle could be that you commit to planning one special date a month.

Our principles help guide us on how we want to live. It can help us get clear on what really matters which helps us save time and energy. We can achieve a lot, especially through small actions by getting clear on our principles.

To get clear on our principles, we should reflect on the following:

- What do you care about and value?

- What are some feelings that you would like to experience?

- What makes you feel anxious or uncomfortable?

Another way to build a new life is to figure out what your purpose is. Our life purpose is not necessarily found in a career or a relationship. It most likely is a lot bigger than just those things.

It takes a lot of work, attention, and effort to figure out your life purpose. It takes a deep understanding of ourselves, our skills, our interests, and the world's needs. It also takes honesty in accepting yourself for who you are and what you bring.

Your life purpose should be natural for you and should come naturally to you.

For example, you might be called to write or called to preach. You don't have to be the greatest at your life's purpose. If you're committed and it brings up certain emotions from you (such as happiness, contentment, and productivity), then you are following your life's purpose. Ultimately, our purpose is to be our best selves, and in turn being our best selves will help others become their best selves.

We also need to find out what we want to do with our lives. We can figure that out by asking these questions:

- What do I find worth suffering for? Who in my life is worth suffering for? What am I okay being uncomfortable for? Who am I okay feeling uncomfortable for?

- What is the best version of myself like? What do they look, act, and feel like?

- If technology or social media did not exist, what would I be doing with my life? What would you be doing with your life if no one was watching? What would you be doing if you did not have anyone to impress?

- What am I naturally good at? What feels natural to do?

- What is my ideal daily schedule? What times do I feel my best?

- What do I want people to remember me for? What do I want people to say or bring up about me?

Chapter Summary

Key Points:

- Connecting with our future highest potential selves can help clarify our goals, the habits we need to implement, and the ways we need to change. It can help us create a plan and tap into our vision of what we want our life to be like, especially since we know what our life could be like.

- Emotional validation is a powerful tool that can help build our relationships with others and with ourselves. Validating our own feelings can be freeing and help us move past them. Validating other people's feelings can help affirm them and build them up.

- We need to get clear on our principles and life purpose. If we do not have our own set of principles, we will end up feeling lost and discontent about life. We will end up chasing or going after goals that do not align or come naturally to us. Having a clear set of principles and a deep awareness of our life purpose can motivate us to become our best selves. It can help motivate us to move forward with confidence and act in the ways that align with our highest selves.

Questions:

- What is your best self like? What do they look and act like?

_____
_____
_____

- What daily habits can you start to become your best self? What actions will I need to take in order to start?

_____
_____
_____

- What feelings do you need to validate? What ways did I act out before because of my feelings not being validated?

_____
_____
_____

Action Plan:

1. Follow the meditation guideline to meet with your highest future self. Spend time talking to and listening to your highest self. Pay attention to the details of your meeting.

2. Journal about and reflect on the details of the meeting. Reflect on the meanings behind your meeting and be sure to take detailed notes on them.

3. Make a list of your life principles. In your list, be sure to explain why these are your life principles

and explain how they can help you create your best life.

4. Create a list of daily habits to start working towards implementing those life principles. Be sure to create a habit for each principle.

Chapter 7: From Self-Sabotage to Self-Mastery

Chapter 7 closes out the book. It covers ways that we can learn how to master ourselves, along with connecting with what brings us joy and happiness.

The chapter starts off by talking about controlling our emotions instead of suppressing them. Buddhists use non-attachment when it comes to mastering the mind. Non-attachment is sitting and letting any feelings that arise come and go. Instead of digging into the feeling, questioning the feeling, or trying to reason out the feeling, we simply accept them and let them go.

Contrary to what some may believe, mastering and controlling your emotions requires letting go of them. We can master our emotions by feeling them and taking note of them. When we suppress our feelings, we give them power over our lives. When we feel our feelings, we learn how to become comfortable with those feelings.

However, if we suppress our feelings, it can make it so that we are fearful of certain feelings and emotions. Being unafraid of our feelings can help us figure out how to respond to them. Because we are not spending time worrying about what our feelings mean or why we feel the way we feel, we are able to use our energy to confront certain feelings.

Suppressing our feelings happens unconsciously while controlling our feelings happens consciously.

Suppressing our emotions can make it so that we do not understand why we are behaving the way we are. It can make it so that you act out those emotions in unexpected or erratic ways. If we learn to control our emotions, we can become more aware of why we are feeling the way we feel and we can figure out how we want to respond to it. The start of self-mastery is simply feeling your emotions and learning how to respond to them.

We can also become mentally strong by trusting ourselves. Trusting ourselves leaves little room for worry, confusion, or regret. It opens us up to inner peace and inner knowing. We can find inner peace by learning to trust that everything will be okay and that we are capable of taking care of ourselves. We must learn to trust that we can handle whatever obstacles come our way. It is trusting that we will return to a baseline, and that we will not be sad, unhappy, or overwhelmed forever.

We can find inner peace by creating goals that align with our values and that align with each other. We need to figure out what will actually make us happy and bring us inner peace. We should not base this on outside opinions or circumstances. We can lose our inner peace overtime due to past trauma or our minds making associations with feelings and outcomes.

We are responsible for finding our inner peace and learning to manage the challenges that come with maintaining it.

We must learn to parent our inner child so that we do not act impulsively or act simply based on unfounded feelings, thus disrupting our inner peace.

We can find our inner peace by becoming aware of our worries, fears, disappointments, and expectations.

We need to tell ourselves that our worries and fears are most likely made up and unlikely to happen. We can take a bigger step by making a list of the following:

- All your previous worries, especially any intense worries. Be sure to be as detailed as possible about the worry and how you felt.

- Every challenge that you said you were incapable of overcoming. Be sure to list what the outcome ended up being.

- All the times you have felt happy and/or inner peace. Be sure to be detailed about what was happening and how you were feeling.

Afterwards, reflect on your responses and take notice of how you feel about them.

We can also gain inner peace by letting go of needing to control things and accepting that most things are outside of our control. We can find inner peace when we let go of the things that make us feel worried.

In order to protect our inner peace, we must also remember that our feelings are not always an accurate representation of what is really happening and what is accurate.

We should never confuse our feelings with being factual. Your feelings can only tell you what your current state of mind is.

They cannot make predictions about the future. We must let go and stop giving into fear. Instead of worrying or overthinking, we must start leaning into our inner peace.

Mental strength plays a key role in our self-mastery. Mental strength is not something we are born with. We must develop our mental strength through time and intention. Mental strength can sometimes come about from very difficult or traumatic situations. Committing to mental strength is a process.

Here's are ways that we can become mentally strong:

- **Create a plan.** Think about the future and plan for it. Think about your goals that you want to achieve, and get comfortable with the thought of achieving them. Creating a plan will help you become more confident and feel less worried about what's to come.

- **Realize that not everything is about you.** Let go of the idea that everyone is secretly thinking about you and judging you. It's simply not true. People are most likely thinking about themselves, and they are not thinking about the "embarrassing" moment you had at dinner.

- **Seek out support.** It is impossible to be good at or knowledgeable about everything. Save yourself time and effort, and ask for help. Seeking out help can also free up your time and bandwidth which can help you work on the things you are good at.

- **Be aware of what you don't know, and don't get caught up in dichotomous thinking.** An example of dichotomous thinking is: if I break up with my partner, I am unlovable. Instead of leaping to an unlikely conclusion, take time to actually think things through. Dissect your dichotomous thoughts by questioning if they are true or if there are other possible outcomes.

- **Stop trying to predict what is going to happen.** Our brains want to predict the future, but the truth is, we can't. We can try to predict it based on past evidence, but it is not possible. We must accept what we don't know and what we can't predict. Instead of spending time trying to predict the future, we should create a plan for it.

- **Take accountability for what has happened and what is happening in your life.** It can be hard to accept, but you are responsible for the outcomes of your life. You are the reason you are experiencing what you are experiencing. When we are aware of the power we have over the outcomes in our life, we can commit to investing in ourselves and doing our best.

- **Process and feel all of your emotions, especially the difficult ones.** Allow your feelings to flow through you without judgment or trying to psychoanalyze yourself. It is important to feel all your emotions in order to fully experience all of them. You will find it hard to notice when you are happy if you never experience sadness. You will find it hard to notice when you are going through a difficult time if you suppress your emotions.

- **Learn from the past, but let it go.** Accept the past for what it is, and figure out how to change the present. You can no longer change what has happened. Instead, we must work on creating our future and making the most out of the present moment. Accepting the past creates space for being fully present here and now.

- **Talk about it.** Don't keep everything in your head or to yourself. Talk to someone. Let it out. You might find that it's less complicated than you initially thought. When we process out loud, especially to others, we will most likely find that we are capable and resourceful enough to overcome and to move forward.

- **Enjoy the journey and take things step-by-step**. Growth takes place in small changes. Don't get so caught up in wanting the future to happen that you miss out on the good of now. You don't have to know all the answers now. Remain present and enjoy yourself.

- **Pay attention to your triggers, but don't act on them.** Our triggers can help us figure out what we need to work on. We don't have to act on our triggers, but we do need to acknowledge and accept them.

- **Feel your discomfort, and don't suppress it.** Discomfort is helpful. Discomfort is trying to teach you something. Use your discomfort to push forward and move towards comfort.

Self-mastery is not all about mental toughness, it is also about enjoying and being happy about your life.

Here are ways to enjoy your life:

- **Stop trying to force yourself to be happy.** Allow happiness to come to you. At our core, we are naturally happy.

- **Be present.** Don't worry about the future or dwell on the past. The present moment is truly a gift that can bring happiness. We'll miss out on this gift by thinking about the past or future.

- **Stop trying to exert control over situations.** You don't have to prove yourself or your worth. You simply have to be. Stop trying to control others or things outside of your control.

- **Lean in to what makes you happy.** Find out what makes you happy – big or small. Soak in all the things that make you happy. Don't overthink what it means to be happy. Instead, simply feel it.

- **Invest in your healthy, positive relationships.** Your relationship can affect the quality of your life. Keep putting into the healthy relationships you have.

- **Keep learning.** Learning helps expand your mind, thoughts, and ideas. Commit to learning as often as possible. Learning can bring a lot of joy and contentment into your life.

- **Rise to the challenge and shift your perspective on them.** Challenges can be great opportunities to build yourself up and to transform.

- **Be aware of how you spend your time.** Recognize what you invest your energy into.

- **Spend time doing nothing.** Take a break.

- **Make time to have fun.** Do things that bring you joy.

To become masters of ourselves, we need to accept the fact that our life is our responsibility.

Life doesn't just happen to us. We play a role in how we respond to what happens to us.

Self-mastery takes time, energy, discipline, and commitment. Becoming our best, highest selves affects us and the people around us. The mountains we climb and conquer will teach us lessons that will help us become our best selves – many times over.

Chapter Summary

Key Points:

- Self-mastery can bring us inner peace. Inner peace is an inner knowing that everything will work out.

- Mental strength is a key component of our self-mastery. We must gain the mental strength to master our thoughts and actions.

- Self-mastery is about fun stuff, too. Self-mastery opens us up to truly enjoying life.

Questions:

- What does inner peace look like for you?

_____

_____

_____

- What parts of your mental state do you want to master? What is holding you back from mastering those parts?

_____

_____

_____

- What brings you joy?

_____

_____

_____

Action Plan:

1. Review the list about mental strength.

2. Take note of and journal about the parts of the list you might find difficult.

3. Create a list of things that bring you joy.

4. Schedule time to do one thing on your joy list.

Background Information About *The Mountain Is You*

The Mountain is You was published by Thought Catalog Books in 2020. Thought Catalog Books is an independently owned organization based in New York and California. The book has 7 chapters and also includes an Introduction.

Background Information About Brianna Wiest

Brianna Wiest lives in Big Sur, California. Wiest is a partner at Thought Catalog Books. Wiest graduated from Elizabethtown College in 2013 with a degree in Professional Writing along with a Gender Studies minor.

She is the author of bestsellers: *101 Essays That Will Change The Way You Think, The Mountain Is You* and *When You're Ready,* and *This Is How You Heal.*

Brianna Wiest's website is https://www.briannawiest.com/. She also has quite a following on Instagram where she shares excerpts of her work.

Trivia Questions

1. What is self-sabotage?

2. What is the upper limit?

3. Who came up with the idea of the upper limit?

4. What is the first step to healing?

5. What is the monkey mind?

6. How does the book explain guilt?

7. What parts of the brain affect how we handle stress?

8. What is adjustment shock?

9. What is extrapolation?

10. How does Wiest describe trauma?

Discussion Questions

1. What are common ways in which we self-sabotage?

2. What does self-mastery mean to you?

3. How do you know when you've found inner peace?

4. What are triggers? How can we use triggers as a tool?

5. What are ways we can validate our feelings? How about other people's feelings?

6. Have you ever experienced a logical lapse? Can you describe what you felt and what happened?

7. Discuss inner child work and your experiences with inner child work.

8. Describe your future highest self. What did you learn from them?

More books from Smart Reads

Summary of Breath: The New Science of a Lost Art By
    James Nestor
Workbook for What Happened to You? By Oprah Winfrey
    and Dr. Bruce Perry
Workbook for Atomic Habits By James Clear
Workbook for Limitless By Jim Kwik
Workbook for The Body Keeps the Score By Dr. Bessel van
    der Kolk
Workbook for Atlas of the Heart By Brené Brown
Workbook for The 48 Laws of Power by Robert Greene

Thank You

Hope you've enjoyed your reading experience.

We here at Smart Reads will always strive to deliver to you the highest quality guides.

So I'd like to thank you for supporting us and reading until the very end.

Before you go, would you mind leaving us a review on Amazon?

It will mean a lot to us and support us creating high quality guides for you in the future.

Thanks once again!

Warmly yours,

The Smart Reads Team

Download Your Free Gift

As a way to say "Thank You" for being a fan of our series, I've included a free gift for you:

Brain Health: How to Nurture and Nourish Your Brain For Top Performance

Go to www.smart-reads.com to get your FREE book.

The Smart Reads Team

Made in the USA
Middletown, DE
03 March 2023

26135532R00036